Mythical Creatures

# GNOMES

Martha London

DiscoverRoo
An Imprint of Pop!
popbooksonline.com

**abdobooks.com**

Published by Pop!, a division of ABDO, PO Box 398166, Minneapolis, Minnesota 55439. 

Printed in the United States of America, North Mankato, Minnesota.

102019
012020

THIS BOOK CONTAINS RECYCLED MATERIALS

Cover Photo: iStockphoto

Interior Photos: iStockphoto, 1, 5, 6–7, 8, 9, 12, 13, 16 (top), 16 (bottom), 29 (top), 30, 31; Shutterstock Images, 10–11, 15, 17 (top), 19, 20 (giant), 20 (nymph), 21 (troll), 21 (human), 21 (top gnome), 21 (fairy), 21 (bottom gnome), 22, 23, 28–29; Interfoto/Alamy, 14; Ian Dagnall/Alamy, 17 (bottom); James Jenkins - Visual Arts/Alamy, 25; Pictures Now/Alamy, 26, 27

Editor: Sophie Geister-Jones
Series Designer: Jake Nordby

**Library of Congress Control Number: 2019942462**

**Publisher's Cataloging-in-Publication Data**

Names: London, Martha, author.

Title: Gnomes / by Martha London

Description: Minneapolis, Minnesota : Pop!, 2020 | Series: Mythical creatures | Includes online resources and index.

Identifiers: ISBN 9781532165788 (lib. bdg.) | ISBN 9781532167102 (ebook)

Subjects: LCSH: Mythical animals--Juvenile literature. | Gnomes--Juvenile literature. | Folklore--Juvenile literature. | Legends--Juvenile literature. | Animals and history--Juvenile literature.

Classification: DDC 398.45--dc23

## WELCOME TO DiscoverRoo!

Pop open this book and you'll find QR codes loaded with information, so you can learn even more!

Scan this code* and others like it while you read, or visit the website below to make this book pop!

**popbooksonline.com/gnomes**

*Scanning QR codes requires a web-enabled smart device with a QR code reader app and a camera.

# TABLE OF CONTENTS

## CHAPTER 1
# HOME IN THE GARDEN

The farmer loved her garden. She planted daisies, lilies, and coneflowers. She placed many gnomes in the flower beds. Each gnome wore a pointy red hat.

WATCH A VIDEO HERE!

*Sir Charles Isham brought garden gnomes to England in the 1840s.*

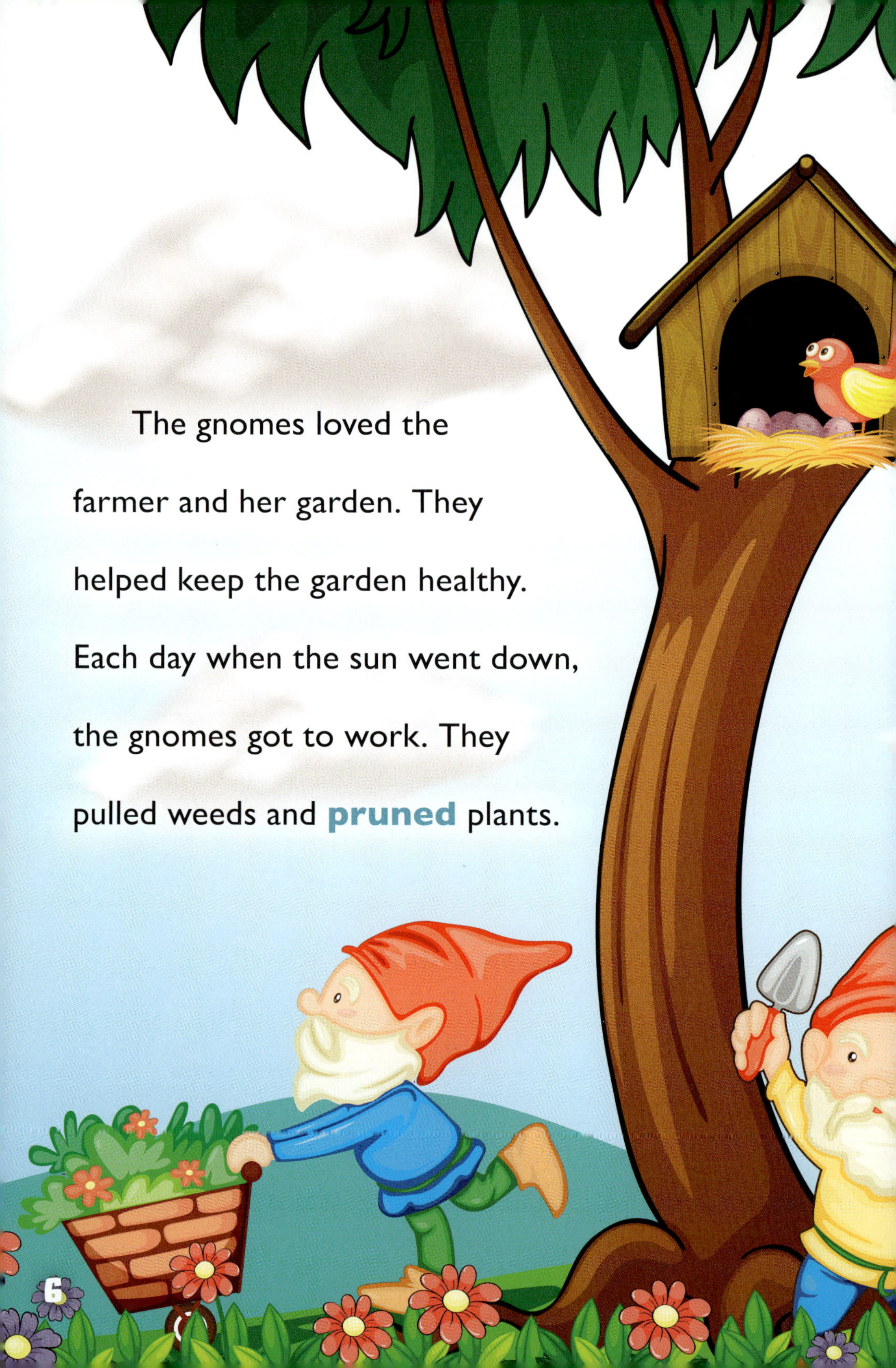

The gnomes loved the farmer and her garden. They helped keep the garden healthy. Each day when the sun went down, the gnomes got to work. They pulled weeds and **pruned** plants.

**DID YOU KNOW?**

*Gnome* comes from a Latin word that means "earth-**dweller**."

*In Norway, there are creatures similar to gnomes called* nisse.

The gnomes worked in the garden all night long. They took care of every plant. When the sun began to rise, the gnomes went back to their spots next to the flowers. The farmer had no idea they were helping her. But her flowers always looked beautiful.

CHAPTER 2

# GNOMES IN HISTORY

Legends about gnomes have existed for hundreds of years. The stories spread across Europe. Many come from Germany, Switzerland, and Sweden. They tell of small creatures that care for the earth.

LEARN MORE HERE!

*Many people believe that gnomes make their homes inside mushrooms or trees.*

Gnomes are very secretive and do not often let people see them in the wild.

It is hard to know what inspired the myths about gnomes. There are not many legends that are just about gnomes. But gnomes often show up in other **folktales**. Gnomes commonly appear in stories about magical forests.

**DID YOU KNOW?**

**Germany has 25 million garden gnomes.**

*Gnomes pay special attention to plants that are growing.*

Sometimes, gnomes are lumped in a group with dwarves, elves, and fairies. But each of these mythical creatures is a bit different. Gnomes are special because of their love for the earth. Unlike other creatures, gnomes are shy. They are not mean. But sometimes they play harmless tricks on people.

## GNOMES OR DWARVES?

Gnomes and dwarves have similar appearances. And they both live underground. But gnomes and dwarves are not the same. Dwarves live in mountains and mines. They work with metal. Legends say they are excellent at making swords and other weapons. Gnomes live in towns and villages. They help with gardening and yard work.

# GNOMES THROUGH THE YEARS

**1500**

A Swiss doctor named Paracelsus first uses the word *gnome* to describe small creatures that live underground.

**1800**

The first garden gnome is made in Germany.

## 1998

*Harry Potter and the Chamber of Secrets* by J. K. Rowling includes stories about gnomes.

## 2018

The movie *Sherlock Gnomes* has gnomes as characters. It retells the famous story of *Sherlock Holmes* by Sir Arthur Conan Doyle.

## 2004

*World of Warcraft* is a fantasy video game that allows players to be gnomes.

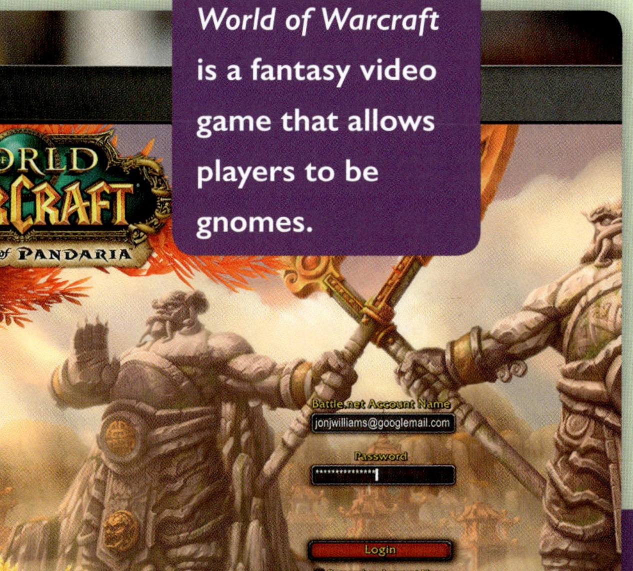

## CHAPTER 3
# FROM WRINKLED TO JOLLY

In early stories, most gnomes were ugly. They had **hunched** backs and wrinkled skin. Even young gnomes looked very old.

COMPLETE AN ACTIVITY HERE!

*Gnomes live much longer than humans do.*

Over time, descriptions of gnomes changed. Today, gnomes often wear pointed red hats. They look friendly. Many have red cheeks, round tummies,

# SIZE COMPARISON

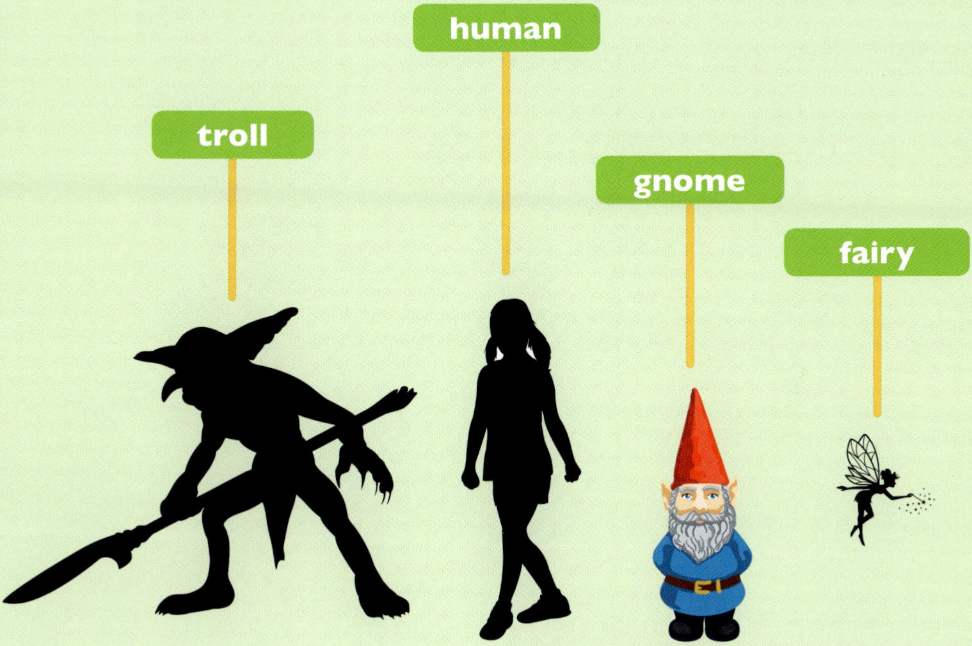

and big smiles. Male gnomes usually have long, white beards.

Gnomes look like very small people. But they have abilities humans do not. **Folktales** say gnomes are very strong, and they have a great sense of smell. Gnomes also know a lot about plants. All of these **traits** help gnomes work in gardens.

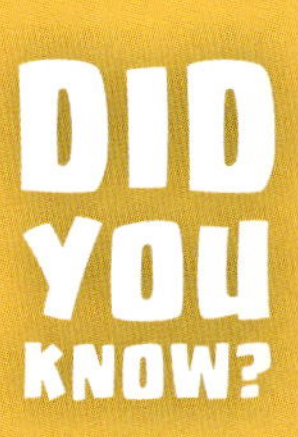


**In 1970, a group of students claimed they saw 60 gnomes at a park in England. They said the gnomes were driving tiny cars.**

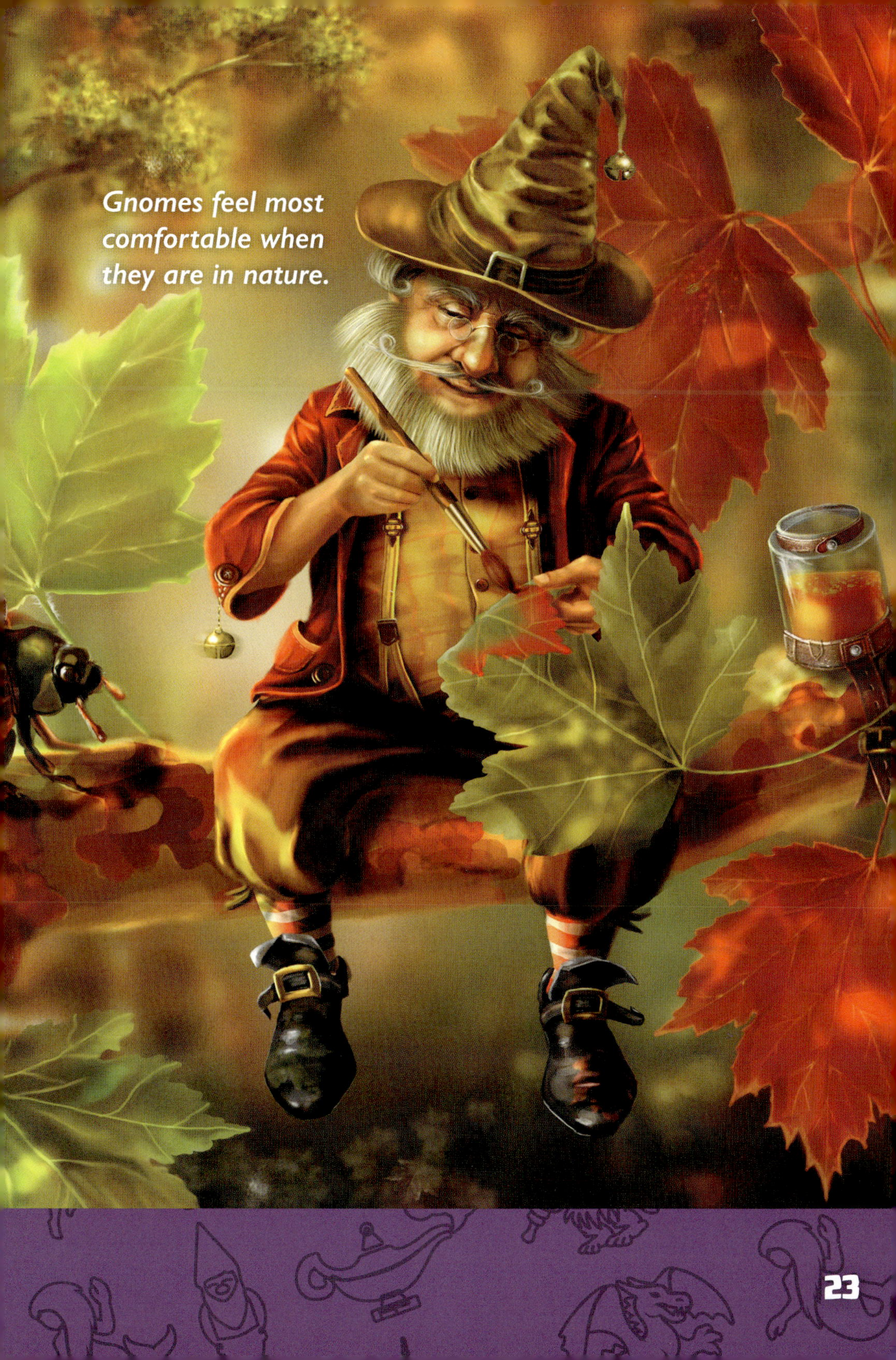

*Gnomes feel most comfortable when they are in nature.*

## CHAPTER 4
# HELPING THE EARTH

In early stories, gnomes were **spirits** that protected the earth. They lived underground. And they guarded the earth's treasures. It was their job to keep the treasures away from humans.

LEARN MORE HERE!

Some myths say that the sun turns gnomes to stone.

*Legends say that gnomes have their own language.*

In these stories, gnomes were not friendly. They played tricks on people. But they took care of plants and animals. Gnomes could move through the ground to help plants grow. As a result, they began to be associated with gardens.

**DID YOU KNOW?**

**Stories say gnomes move through dirt as easily as fish swim through water.**

By the 1800s, gnomes were considered lucky. Legends said some were companions to famous **inventors** and artists. They were helpful creatures. People started putting statues of gnomes

in their gardens. Some people still use these decorations today.

*Dutch legends say that gnomes taught people how to make shoes.*

# MAKING CONNECTIONS

## TEXT-TO-SELF

What would you do if you saw a gnome?

## TEXT-TO-TEXT

Gnomes often appear in stories about dwarves, elves, or fairies. Have you read about any of these creatures? What did you learn?

## TEXT-TO-WORLD

Many legends about gnomes began in northern Europe. Can you think of a legend that comes from a different part of the world?

# GLOSSARY

**dweller** – a creature that lives in a specific location.

**folktale** – a made-up story about a place's history.

**hunched** – bent over.

**inventor** – someone who creates new things.

**prune** – to take off the dead parts of a plant.

**spirit** – a creature that is not human or animal and is probably magical.

**trait** – a physical quality that a creature or plant has.

# INDEX

Scan this code* and others like it while you read, or visit the website below to make this book pop!

popbooksonline.com/gnomes

*Scanning QR codes requires a web-enabled smart device with a QR code reader app and a camera.